unsettled

© Harry Laing 2021

Also by Harry Laing

Thirst (Phoenix Press, 1993)
Backbone (Bunda Press, 2010)

for children

Shoctopus (Bunda Press, 2015)
MoonFish (Ford Street, 2019)
RapperBee (Ford Street, 2021)

This book is copyright. Apart from any fair dealing for the purposes of study and research, criticism, review, or as otherwise permitted under the Copyright Act, no part may be reproduced in any manner without first gaining written permission from the author.

ISBN: 978-1-877010-96-5

Walleah Press
1/4 Floreat Crescent
Trevallyn
Tasmania 7250 Australia
ralph.wessman@walleahpress.com.au

Cover by Askepott Design
Set in Sabon 10.5/15.0 by Ralph Wessman
Printed by IngramSpark, Melbourne

unsettled

Harry Laing

Contents

The heart is not two places

A Scot returns to Braidwood	3
Life rewound	6
Dog-time (almost) gone	7
Parachuted into a primary school for a creative writing workshop	8
Not going quietly	9
Wood goes round	10
Spinebills	11
Two moons	12
Gang-gangs are family	13
Crossed paths	15
The appearance of a leech	16
Born again	18

unsettled

1822	27
Art Gallery of South Australia	28
After landing at Westernport Bay	29
Speculation	30
And then there was Batman	31
Willie's rocks	32
With William Robertson	33
Buckley, but who is Buckley?	34
Buckley's Bream	35
The Barrabool Hills	36

And in no time	37
It seems William R developed a bull neck	38
Extracted from the *Hobart Mercury* 1872	39
Died 1874, worth £290,000	41

Talking road

invocation	45
you take it	46
the road as homeopathy	47
rodomontade	48
roadkill	49
will you speed up or move over you	50
now you become aware the hills	51
road-eaters	52
Lockhart Jerilderie reverie	53
get out of the car	54
time flows present to past	55
silos	56
driving to distraction	57

Narcissus is us

Less is more	61
Dental diatribe	62
Tatt attack	64
What's in a name?	66
Hair, hair	68
Doodling dogs	70

Shaving	72
Touch the silence	74
Narcissus is us	76

What's cooking?

we're going up	81
the overthinking and the heated minds	82
unmoored untethered glare	83
tipping point talk	84
carbon copies	85
and tonight...	86
the entire country inflamed	87
headlong (with Icarus)	88
more more	89
flare	90
but where are the snows of yesteryear?	91
spooked	92
look out to sea	93
history happens faster now	94
crowing	95
I'm not granite	98
the mountains have a certain look	99

To Gerard

The heart is not two places

A Scot returns to Braidwood

1

I take a Highland river
its peat-coloured water,
muscular water
poured through the Streens
and smoothed into pools at Dulsie.
I take the glassy ribs of the Findhorn River
from under Ballacrochan where my grandfather fished
and I'll pack them now
along with that last long Scottish evening
the grain of it
and the slant of the light
something to remember.

2

Flying at night is an easy illusory glide
that creates no ripple.
A cosseted shuttle, playing at weightless
the bleary game of drifting unslept
in transit from gate to gate
without apparent effort.

Body folded, mind suspended
in the quiet roar of engines, or
the sound of a river pouring itself
away.

3

At the twitch of a window shade
the world rolls over. Winter.
The endless clean dawn
of Australia opening a salt-rimmed eye.

Such exquisite desert vacancy
startles at this height
and I have no words to articulate
the look of the white pans,
their circlets of salmon-tinted cloud,
the red and roadless age of this country.

I feel that frisson pitched
between thrill and fear
of being unknown here,
of having body and bagful of Europe
and Scotland taken off me
somewhere back there
in the nowhere night.

4

Landed
I find I am tissue thin.

Travelling, it seems,
carries no weight.

No trace of where I've been –
no pointers, standing stones or spires.

This light, so raucous
so in-your-face eager

the trees' crazy waving
the anarchist birds and their shouting
in fact everyone's throat just opens
and whatever they want to say
spills out.

5

One sleep here,
and the distance between hemispheres
has set solid.
The other, now unreachable
but still fresh
like a skin stepped out of.

Seeing crisp white plane-trails
in this southern sky
I think I can leap back
like a salmon up river.

But that firm handwriting
turns out to be cottonwool
one-way only.

When will I learn
the heart is not two places?

Life rewound

unburied
unburnt
unpensioned
unlearnt

unwept
unmissed
unread
unkissed

unshouted
undrunk
unguilty
unsunk

unsaid
undone
unbroken
unborn

Dog-time (almost) gone

*from hour to hour, we ripe and ripe
and then from hour to hour we rot and rot
and thereby hangs a tale…*
        As You Like It, Act 2, Scene VII

Starting with the dog-clock
the clock of our dog's life
and the vet talking dud kidneys
saying if our dog was human she'd be a hundred

and I wasn't listening
just feeling a dull thud behind the ribs
like the smiling vet had cracked me one
a dog-life gone quicker than you could bark

from the moment we picked her up
two months and two hands long
she's been gobbling it all down

the pup-years tearing boxes and books to shreds
jumping like she needed out of everywhere
prancing with sticks, a mock-snarling
one-dog-circus, a plant-pot doyenne

now who's creeping down the steps
with a wondering look and the silver face
and the back legs not quite obedient
as if she left something behind
what could that be?

Parachuted into a primary school
for a creative writing workshop

A lesson in keeping your age at bay
all the tiny chairs tell me
and the many heads of the child animal
bent over tables
and amazing to say they're writing quietly
and I've slipped a toe into that river of young life,
all those green bones flowing
                        through the classroom walls
out into the playground sea
the possibility shining from thirty faces
as they turn again to me
whatever they reckon I am
a silver-haired pencil, one hand of a clock
it doesn't matter
I'm getting younger and younger

just standing here.

Not going quietly

A man can feel a deep unease
surrounded by a wall of trees
their silent-ranked conspiracies –

dropping branches on a whim
seedlings marching closer in
all this *growing* aimed at *him*.

A man will feel no hesitation
when threatened by the vegetation
to bring noise into the equation.

That's why chainsaws were designed –
to give men back their peace of mind.

Wood goes round

*Ash was tree
and time was crushed
wind stirred ash
a tree blew down*

the stone was broken
tree split stone
its roots divided
granite's tongue

the chainsaw wails
the splitter bites
wood piled up
the tree submits

time steps in
and seasons wood
words dry up
the woodpile laid

feed the fire
heat the water
drive the house
the length of winter

*ash was tree
and time was crushed
wind stirred ash
a tree blew down.*

Spinebills

Sickle beaks for sipping work
nectar tingling on the tongue

> *jinking for a hit of sugar*
> *crank the world up crank it over*

trim in chestnut, crisp in cream
first to whistle after rain

> *jinking for a hit of sugar*
> *crank the world up crank it over*

chip chip song sung upside down
blossom-dodgers, zig-zag clowns

> *jinking for a hit of sugar*
> *crank the world up crank it over.*

Two moons

1

First the surprise:
late summer's eye-opener
you rising full and fat above Currockbilly
lifting all that dark country
and I want you to stay right there,
molten
world hanging off you
the way you handle my astonishment
so consummately.

2

And the other one
the one I've missed without knowing
your absence meaning
some perturbation
things out of kilter
then I catch you low in the sky
sharp as an intake of breath
pin-point, slim, crispest lineation
what gets me every time
when you are brand new
how things are set right
how I am too.

Gang-gangs are family

Seeing the flare on the road
the pang of it and the flame colour of the head
extinguished
slow down for the dead gang-gang

how many years, decades undone
no shift left in him
breath banged out of the feathers

having not turned fast enough
too easily tossed aside

the indifference of the road to my picking him up
laying him down under a hawthorn

watched
by three grey shapes
his widow
        the two others

*

Gang-gangs are family
witness to your comings and goings
they've been around for ever

wondering how you could fail to understand
what they're saying which hinges on…
when you say creaking door and other rusty epithets
you're nowhere near

easier to translate the crooning they get up to
rubbing shoulders in branch position
a nod from the male to show off the pom-poms
of his geranium-coloured headdress

or should that be salmon, flame, cherry
they're all wrong
so give up trying to describe the colour the sound
and watch them feeding close-up
raining down green wattle-seed

before they're off calling again
a sound that never fails to stand the ranges
on their heads

a sound that puts you back where you belong.

Crossed paths

The nature of this place –
what you don't see coming.
Bark sprouts a beak and a rock shifts –
suddenly the dirt has spikes
and a dark chocolate face.

Ripple of an echidna
quiverful of blond spines
and plodding insouciance
the intent of him, his nose going in
going in.

I shouldn't approach but I do
and he stops, knowing there's something extra
something he doesn't need
and being all muscle but also a little fearful
or perhaps having the ear of the dirt
he digs in and sinks instantly.

My dog barks stupidly
and the island of echidna trembles
a soft soul under all that armour.

so I back off, give his quills some room
watch that beady nose untuck like a baton
and conduct him on his way again.

The appearance of a leech

You flagrant straining thing
        one end anchored
                the other tracing your desires in the air

finger in black neoprene
        doorstep apparition
                weaving figure-of-eights
                      in a blind and blatant ode to blood

bodies are what turn you on
        mine sends your head spinning
                I'm warm   full   grippingly near

I pluck your insinuating self
        and roll it between finger and thumb
                which turns my stomach over

a squashed-berry sensation
        both wet and obscene

oh I've stumbled on you before
        dancing on the gear stick of the car
                sucking the dog's lip
                      kissing our pillow

your swollen bladder
        inching sideways from a feast
                trailing the red evidence

I flick you away   repulsed
       now stay put in your little pit of leaves
             or wherever it is you lurk and twist
                   this time bloodless.

Born again

Writing you back
when I can't ring
can't say anything

writing you back
stretches something between us
when the cord you kept pulling
that connection's gone slack

so I'm writing you back, Dad
I've found your address
in these poems.

1. *Born again*

in a blue plastic apron
potting plants under direction.
You're a shuffle-man in slippers
though still carefully buttoned
into your old-time manners.

Such a gentleman they call you
and I think *little do they know*
but why bring that up now, in here
where no one's got a grip on what they were...

Besides your name has changed,
once Andy, you're Andrew now.
Perhaps you *are* a new man
I can't believe the photographs I'm shown
you party-hatted, downing cake
dancing, for God's sake,
with some old dear you might
in your right mind have called a *bag*.

And now you think we might get served
in this convenient hostelry
and make your gentlemanly signal to a carer
meaning *how about a cup of tea?*

Matron says *he remembers more about the future
than he does about the past*

which makes sense, at least to me –
I think you've always had your eye on this
your second infancy.

2. *Full circle*

Some homing instinct brought you back –
we used to live just streets away
Camilla House, the same high ceilings,
cornices, bay windows, in other words respectable
that other life behind you now.

You shrug your room off saying *is this mine?*
It's dark in here smells slightly medical
the soft toys on your bed are ogling me
you gesture at a teddy bear and scowl
I don't know how that infiltrated here.

My only compass point's Aunt Janet
smiling from that wartime photo
the one you saved from fire and winos.

Let's head into the garden
find you a fag
we'll take our scraps of sky together.

Nothing you've ever owned has stuck
but landing here now that's some luck.

3. *Rings no bells*

When I ring you ask
But Harry, why are you ringing?
To see how you are
But why are you ringing?
Has it been snowing?
But why are you ringing?
What about frost?
But why are you ringing?
Did you go for a walk?
But why are you ringing?
I live in Australia
Because I am married
But why are you ringing?
Twenty years now
But why are you ringing?

4. *Escape from Camilla House*

Restless
it's the rhythm cramped in your legs
your mind in forward motion –

dressed for a quick exit
you're stationed here at the glass front door
in jacket, waistcoat, tie, brushed hair

so when visitors enter
you simply slide out on a little wave
of politeness, a professional job
and no-one to see it.

Out on the street
freedom seems longer and higher
you make your way
using the old walls as eyeholds
hesitant at crossings
the sky tiring itself in too many directions.

Tramping in slippers,
a soreness in your feet and your mind
the city unravels you, it's a fog
it's a gaggle of cops
who appear to be friendly despite the old alarm bells
of *what have I done?*
you answer *Andrew Laing.*

Safely back in your room
you light up the cigarette you managed to extract
and inhale and it's sweet to feel tired
just this once

and that, Dad, is the fire alarm blaring
and this is the second time you've done a runner
and Matron has a breakdown shortly after.

unsettled

1822

A respectable looking date
tying its cravat taking a little bow
talking pioneers, capital, land grants.

1822   the Robertson brothers William and John
arrive in Van Diemen's Land on the Regalia
young men like coiled springs
sons of the Scottish diaspora
taking up acres on the Elizabeth River
where they toil stock breed
toil stock breed

>   (words that sound like gunshots)

so from here on
I'm bracketing everything –

>   (1831, the profit they made selling land
>   the emporium begun in Hobart
>   *Melrose*, my gt gt gt grandfather's house
>   in Battery Point
>   1831, the Black War raging)

close brackets, open ears
dates are not innocent
not ivory counters on a board
dates are doors that swing open
revealing truth that can't be forgotten.

Art Gallery of South Australia

Four Robertsons arranged in a square
the focus of the wall
William, Margaret, brother John, daughter Jessie
and I'm casting a line across water and time
making a ripple in the gallery calm
weather banished here
no squalls off the Southern Ocean
nothing to stir the temple air
no dirt certainly no blood
nothing to ruffle these ivory faces
the past so carefully lit
contrast the velvet black of coats and cravats
and the whiteness of their faces
with Manalargenna gazing close by
his red ochre and pipeclay dreads
Bock's gouache eerily alive
and already the tide's slipping in fast
there's more than a ripple here
there's a shiver.

After landing at Westernport Bay

William walks to Port Phillip
so how did it look?
I wish I had his eyes of 1836

> *to see that country laid out*
> *in swamps in chains of ponds*
> *lagoons peering through bulrush fingers*
> *swans' soft honking from dark water*

on round Corio Bay he goes
where the You Yangs hold up the sky
I wish I had his eyes of 1836

> *to see that country laid out*
> *in swamps in chains of ponds*
> *lagoons peering through bulrush fingers*
> *the swans' soft honking from dark water*

was there a moment
he forgot what he was doing
a moment the country walked him?

Speculation

Van Diemen's Land the shape of a heart
boom and bust rippling through the arteries
shores tightening with pressure

speculation pumping away
sending a wave across Bass Strait
that rolls swiftly back
with grass in its mouth

grass wave on grass wave
sending men frantic for Port Phillip
what they haven't seen
tastes sweeter than anything

that body of land over the water
magnet for capital
grass rumour stitched up as fact

and always more over the water
always more.

And then there was Batman

Livewire   persuader
also *rogue, thief, cheat, liar*
                    according to Glover
Batman the quivering compass needle
Port Philip his true north
Australia Felix his tawny-headed mistress
her skirts her plains her grasses
her very few inhabitants

*murderer of blacks and the vilest man
I've ever known* (Glover again)
Batman offering himself as go-between
and the necessity of taking land gently
along the lines of a treaty

and William Robertson
finger stubbed on the map
name pencilled over a large holding
puts up half the cash for Batman's expedition
points out the Yarra for landing

I see William with iron legs   a sturdy vessel
his mind stocked with possibilities
boiling over with impatience

Batman the bridge over Bass Strait
his character   better leave that one behind
draw the curtain.

Willie's rocks

Up the rutted track to Dunachton
so this is where he came from
quintessential Highlands of Scotland
a straggle of birch, the modest burn
a damp place, green and folded-in
the remains of a croft or two
outlines in stone, a hill of rock behind
he would have stooped to the door here
I'm not surprised he wanted more
from cramped skies and miserable landlords
the man had expansion written in his bones
his craving to walk out wide beyond Alvie
the Spey Valley, kick over the traces
spurred by the birch
the ticking muscle in the rock
the burn's cajoling
some need got into him
some shift some calling.

With William Robertson

Here we are on the Western Plains,
1836, I can't say where exactly
the country untroubled by white names
I'm struck by his solidity
like he's been quarried out of bluestone

and the yellow stars of yam daisy
the jutting heads of a line of bustard
the kangaroo grass to the knees
the teal lifting off the lagoon
that tussock wind from the west
and the vocabulary of volcanic humps

William and I looking west
only the grass heads rustling
clear on his broad face the fact
the tussock wind blows no meaning
the duck only good for eating
it seems all he wants to do
is stuff land and cattle down his leg-bones.

Buckley, but who is Buckley?

Escaped convict, returned ghost
call him anything you like
nothing sticks to Buckley
his long form edging out of vision

after thirty years with the Wadawurrung
he stumbles back into view
I say stumbled, how did he appear
the sounds he made, what were they?

English gone
could only point to his tattoo
sun moon **WB** and when bread was offered
remembered the word *bread*

and behind the word
the food he'd gathered for thirty years
under a different sun and moon
bone-memory, that country
tucked behind the vast brow

Buckley described as
always discontented and dissatisfied
torn down the middle

riding back to the Wadawurrung people
the saddle-high grasses whispering to him

who he really is.

Buckley's Bream

There were so many they filled the river
at Karaaf, Bream Creek
full tide and full moon
pouring up and down
a river-muscle of bream
silver surface you could walk over
Buckley making his traps
waiting for the tide to turn
then pulling in the bream
I dreamed it, a brimming dream
Buckley's long shape by the river
the glint of pre-lapsarian light
on Karaaf, Bream Creek
Buckley taking the rain off the ocean
waiting for the bream
a dream of Buckley
the bream and the brimming.

The Barrabool Hills

Buckley said, must have said
they were his, did he own them
how could he, who gave them?

Let's start that again
Buckley said they were his
given to him by Barrabool Wadawurrung
he gave them to William Robertson

hearsay or fantasy, family memory
William was tramping Westernport to Corio
and Buckley sees William with two packs
(Gellibrand couldn't carry his own)
William had brawn and Buckley admired him
believe what you like

> *the Barrabool Hills, meaning hills-down-to-water,*
> *hills shaped like oysters*

William's nose twitching, his pockets impatient
wanting them badly

but the hills shook their heads
slipped his hands
shucked his brand

> *the Barrabool Hills, meaning round*
> *meaning hills-down-to-water,*
> *hills shaped like oysters.*

And in no time

sheep and human mouths began tearing
the breath out of the land

blue-chinned squat-stone men
settled on the water
drew their boundaries tight

building names with acres
        while the land looked away
                and the sky fell

in no time
the meaning of the land
        was the owning of the land
                was the moaning of the land

was all owned land
        but not home land
home always elsewhere
        back there

this land, grass-land
        disappearing into the many mouths
                and the sound of swamps unspooling

grubbed grubbed grubbed
        the sound of tearing.

It seems William R developed a bull neck

The daguerreotype delivers a shock...

so that's him   *and he's ugly*
the width of the neck with its bulging veins
he could be a prizefighter

nothing like Bock's early portrait
or was that a carefully cultivated lie
the mythical slender gent with ivory skin
carefully concealed neck and small chin

is this daguerreotype the truth
or simply what happens to men like him
who drive their own fortune
men who take the bull by the horns
tough souls born with hooves
drumming those hooves on the land

trampling you might say
no wonder the patriarch ends up bull-necked.

Extracted from the *Hobart Mercury* 1872

Upon taking up permanent residence in Colac,
Mr Robertson acted with his usual promptitude
waged an unceasing war with thistles
filled up the wombat holes
shot and trapped rabbits without cessation

Mr Robertson never stopped
thanks to a strong hand
and a **green old age**

no, it didn't take long

**Mr Robertson acting with his usual promptitude
has not been much troubled by the long ears**
not much troubled by the rabbits, no
the wombats ditto

it didn't take long
for the **English grasses** to establish themselves
or his **imported Herefords and Durhams**

and the Gulidjan people
was he troubled by them
in his **permanent residence**
filling his paddocks with **English grasses**
dividing them between his six sons and daughters

**acting with his usual promptitude
without cessation
into his green old age**

as for the time before rabbits
                      before thistles
                                      before Robertsons

nothing to be troubled by.

      (Bolded excerpts from *Hobart Mercury*, 1872.)

Died 1874, worth £290,000

William was an honest man
acquired his land at auction
what did the land say?

> *Gulidjan, Wadawarrung*

Herefords and Shorthorns
William after pedigree
what did the land say?

> *Gulidjan, Wadawarrung*

he bred a stately tonnage
and the bulls were beauties
what did the land say?

> *Gulidjan, Wadawarrung*

Oxford Cherry Duke
worth 19,000 guineas
what did the land say?

> *Gulidjan, Wadawarrung*

land that was trampled
land made his fortune
what did the land say?

> *Gulidjan, Wadawarrung*

Talking road

road for grit
road for bone
road for pointing
road for home
road for ready
road for bust
road for shreds of tyre-crust
road for roaring
road for lags
road for drifters
road that drags
road-emotion
road wells up
road the killer
road the truck
road for nothing
road for slack
road the reason
no road back

you take it

the road's offer
and in the days before you go
the ground under you stirs

> *distance intrudes*
> *looking lengthens*
> *ranges soften*

the mind's grown wheels
you're filling up with country
running your hand over its folds and river-nerves

> *distance intrudes*
> *looking lengthens*
> *ranges soften*

the ground under you stirs
and the solids of your life shiver
in anticipation

> *distance intrudes*
> *looking lengthens*
> *ranges soften*

the road as homeopathy

the freeway the artery
feeling the pulse of the country
bloodstream of trucks hauling
lettuces IPads roof-trusses
and people like molecules
all bent on somewhere in bubbles sealed units
no taking the air no dog on the tuckerbox
making our own atmosphere
firmly behind glass
while the tea-tree waves madly
full-blossom-foaming
grass bows to slipstream
hills nod in passing
we're taking the load any load
cement runs like velvet under the wheels
no reasons needed
our nomadic tuning

rodomontade*

road-bragger
corner-digger
roadeo-rider
pedal-warrior
slow-car-rooter
rev-head-rumour
swear-and-passer
stick-on-the-arser
slew-and-squealer
(future-stealer)
heart-rate-ramper
soundtrack-cranker
road-avatar
road-olator
road-orator

road-high-roller

* A brag, a boast; an extravagantly boastful or arrogant remark or speech

roadkill

singular plural and impersonal word
for the splayed the sprawled the scattered
rib-bits and skin-scraps of creatures
like the aftermath of war
all those feet stuck in the air
the smears of blood on the deck

you'd think they'd learn
at least have some inkling
but they keep coming
powered by dusk and dawn
one generation after another
bouncing into the headlights

suicidal in any language
and we've seduced them
with our clean hard road
sliced through their domain
the roar they don't hear
speed they can't measure

it's carnage, car-collateral
we ride the road
they pay the toll

will you speed up or move over you

steady-goers
corner-slowers
hesitators
teen L-platers
80 k'ers
fast-lane-stayers
highway-creepers
would-be-sleepers
constant brakers
ancient shakers
baby-touters
Sunday-outers
cockie-dawdlers
haybale-haulers
weaving texters
heaving sexters
Winnebagers
convoy stagers
diesel-spewers
gravel-slewers
speed-impeders
temper-needlers
road-rage-feeders

I am a man
the road is mine
and I'll arrive
ahead of time

now you become aware the hills

you've been riding are falling behind
and the road has no need to flex its muscle
settling for slow bends and the level run

under the spell of sideways gravitation
and the constant tug of the plain
the hills have dwindled to ridges

west of Wagga
The Rock a last vertical reminder
shark's tooth jagged into Wiradjuri sky
beyond that more spacious   flatter than you remember

sweetness and intimacy
this country's body
its offer of expansion

road-eaters

pulled up at the servo
you see the true road-eaters
hauled out of their car-element
unsure they should be vertical
displaying glassy smiles
dazed by the accumulation of distance
not the kind to linger while filling up
assiduously shifting windscreen-smear
having tacitly agreed
ten minutes no more
hovering inside over pie and chips
he steers the sauce round the plate
pumps the pedal under the table
their shoulders blurred
her tea with no words
stuffed with kilometres
hungry for road
there's nothing much to add
married as they are
to the white lines

Lockhart Jerilderie reverie

in-between country
compass set to the mood you're in
elements of gate and mailbox
dust plume from some track
the squatting sky
the space that steals your words
towns strung out like beads
you count them off
Lockhart with the lidded-eyes
Urana where the iron spider watches
Jerilderie where the jokes are made of tin

in-between country which understands you perfectly
like the crop-duster plane
flying so low
nothing needs explaining

get out of the car

get out of the car
you don't need a reason

get out of the car
grow silence   a new limb

get out of the car
your knots have all gone

get out of the car
the cracked dirt is grinning

get out of the car
start again here

time flows present to past

like I'm driving backwards
could so easily slip
between the ribs of the black box the boree
and never be seen again

Birrang: country shifting about on emu feet late afternoon
slow-creek-water-winking

Birrang: seeing by slant-light
when the vegetation has body
the horizon's tawny-gold reach into black cloud

and I'm barrelling along present to past
listening to The Pretenders

don't get me wrong

silos

    Kulwin
    Tiega
    Galah
    Torrita
    Linga
    Boinka
    Tutye
    Cowangie
    Panitya
    Parilla
    Parrakie
    Jabuk
    Peake
mallee-risers with cathedral possibilities though close
up they wear tin hats not bell towers a tangle of chutes
and bung-ugly concrete cylinders but for a moment
laying aside the railway and the speck-settlements in this
country all verticals are monuments give or take the grain

driving to distraction

sure I get into trouble the lure the allure of just looking
the eye's hooked I'm all eye wanting to cram it in the
lie of the land who lives here mailbox cattle roof what's
behind and beyond I can understand why my passenger
doesn't appreciate my head at 90° to the road but it's got
a life of its own I can't stop never have anyway my hands
are on the wheel the car knows exactly trust me
what a fat stretch of roadside water and smattering of
baby cypress pine I'm riveted by that brown falcon with
the dark eye flying to the creek via that buffer of open
space and near in the waving spear grass and again the
flooded box trees see what I mean so it goes

Narcissus is us

Less is more

When cars are driverless
and swimming pools diver-less

when Boxing Day's test-less
and gyms are chest-less

when soccer is bootless
and orchards are fruitless

when rivers are waterless
and wars are slaughter-less

and forests treeless
and lamp posts pee-less

and skies are bird-less
and sewers turd-less

and leaf-blowers noiseless
and toy-guns boy-less

when surf is wave-less
and men are shave-less

and kitchens cook-less
and libraries book-less.

Dental diatribe

Life is a grind
just ask my teeth

at night you'll find them
pitched against each other
like pliers says the dentist

it seems I'm a nocturnal bone-crusher
a circus-performer hanging by my teeth

but what would I know, I'm asleep

unconscious of this jaw-war
tooth against tooth
splintering chips, fissures and cracks
two tonnes of pressure per square inch
says my dentist lightly

anyway he's made me pivots, they clip on
they're like blue plastic boats
buffers, platform shoes in my mouth
and I hate them

goodnight is now   *goo-nigh*
but at least we're equal
my wife has her own set
she's a clencher
goo-nigh

what a pair
I never thought I'd see this day
wha dib you pay?

I never thor....

goo-nigh

goo-nigh ma dar-wi

goo-nigh

Tatt attack

Like something best left underground
to writhe and moan   with Gothic roots
black bootlace writing

what strange tectonic shift of fashion
has freed this thing which morphs and breeds
runs feral everywhere you look
tyre-tracks, claws and scales
knots, zigzags, jig-jags, cars, dragons, flowers
slathered on ten million virgin arms and legs

tatts   that's what I'm getting at
tatts   we're under tatt-attack

you're branded, kids
the indelible whim that blew through your mind
and joined with your flesh
won't be shrugged off

all those wincing hours taken
to defame good skin with ink
what did you think with your chain-linked sleeves
and armoured calves

and what about skin
it's a beautiful thing   let it alone
let it bloom   let it be
written-in weathered-in   skin
slept in   kissed and well-kept   skin

now swirls and dashes and zigs and zags
and dogs and cars and flowers and skulls

here let me hand you a mirror, Jackson
this is your nursing home future
those demons inked up your arms
are not breathing fire now
they're slack-tongued
they're chalk and paper
and the snakes on your legs have sagged very badly
keep pushing that wheelie

look   Breanna's got something to show you
her necklace of skulls   a little bit wilted
at eighty-three

so think, kids
before you get inked
think of the lick of the years
and the way things shrink

beauty might be in the eye of the beholder
but tatts don't get better as they get older

so keep your skin unwritten on
shun the needle-man

leave those tatts where they belong   underground
to writhe and moan.

What's in a name?

I don't want names to get too bland
new parents need a gentle hand

here's a useful little list
for namers needing class and grist.

Let's start with the Bible
so healthy-violent, so tribal

if it's a boy how about *Cain?*
(I'm sure he won't do it again!)

and if a girl try *Jezebel*
as nobody now believes in hell

I like *Tobit, Job* and *Lot*
though *Onan's* sadly been forgot

all sonorous and biblical
now let's move to medical

Ebola, a girl, how sweet
and *Zika* out there on the street

Statins for a healthy male
is *Catscan* beyond the pale?

Anna Phylaxis: two in one
Stent a boy who'd have some fun

and moving swiftly on to food
where names are nourishing and good

if your boy's a little prick
you could call him *Turmeric*

Kale is muscular and green
Pancetta elegant and lean

best of all food-names by far (for girls)
is *Chia* followed by *Quinoa*

now zooming in on Google Earth
what about a girl called *Perth*?

follow my geographical drift
with boy names: *Lava, Rio, Rift*

I'll finish there, that's quite enough
parents, call your newborn *Stuff.*

Hair, hair

I'm in recession
my hair is waving goodbye politely and whitely
tide that won't come back in
shiny banks of scalp exposed
I dreamt it was brown last night
under the white the white the white

once I had a stack, dark-brown-black
a thicket, like wire
my assumption my forest my crown my proof
of youth

look at this thin stuff,
these white wings that blow up in the wind
I've got the tuft, the island left behind
I'm in recession
baldness, male pattern
I'm taking the tonsure, moving to monk
is that me in the mirror?
my hairdresser fans what little she can
left or right
to cover the fact, the lack

some men step up to the gun
and shear it all off
mug-bravado!
shave your head and you're Chopper Read,
a neck from League, bulb, a punk and a crim
too much nose and shiny cranium
those ugly bumps and lugs behind that shouldn't be seen

keep what you have I say
take comfort from this mantra, *sparsity is power*
all the men at the top are going back
tufted and stippled, the plucked chook look
their naked thrust no longer disguised
those frontal lobes exposed...

Oh and memo to the fools in their forties
who think a lick of gel is good
who cultivate the lifted duck
the glistening tent...

there's nothing to be done
unless you're Elton John
that grinning transplant victim

yes what I've got is going
I just hope my recession rate is slowing
I don't like that new feeling
the tingling up top
reminded by the sun
to distribute the block

how did I get here
envying the young dudes' hair
the way it hangs or stands
thick and dark, lank or greased
they've no idea the tide of hair goes out for everyman
waving whitely

goodbye goodbye...

Doodling dogs

There's oodles of 'em
doodle-dogs, noodle-defying dogs
not just your twisted bitzers
I'm talking high-end ritzy listers
labradoodles and spoodles
cavoodles and boodles and floodles

look there's a shitsoodle
shitsu crossed chopstick
blitzed with rat
did I just step on that?

What about the woodle
a grim Scottish dog
wolfhound crossed with electric blanket
coat the texture of thistle
colour of aged whisky
drinks itself under the carpet
and is the carpet

or how about ze groodle
blond Russian hound with KGB curly coat
and Novichok nerve poison on collar

not forgetting the floodle
a little French yap yap
wiz its own pink jacket and cap
and shampooed paws and come for kiss kiss
having done piss piss on your floor

and the stroodle, ze German Shepherd
crossed wiz der apfel hund
nice and spicy wiz ze big feet
und massive ears and tendency to
put paws on your shoulders
and breathe wurst in your face

then the Brexit hound
the BorisoodleJohnsonpoodle
three-legged liar of a dog
limping off into the sunset…

And finally
the Aussie Oodnadattaoodlebattler
Kelpie crossed Bull Arab jumped
by a dingo out of a foxie
cut with cattle dog
back o' the ute, chain-snapper
works all weather takes heat by the throat
bites the arse off bulls
demolishes yards
and dreams how it's got real class.

Shaving

A man's day is measured in bristle.
I grow darker by the hour.
The clock of stubble ticks, it itches
and nags.
I need the blade and I need it bad.
I hear my father snorting *you haven't shaved!*
If I tried growing the stuff beyond a day
it would be a whiter shade of grey
moth-eaten, raggedy,
not George Clooney.

So let hipsters duel strong-beardedly
only a shave will do for me.

There was a teenage time when all I wanted
was to scrape my face and be a man,
miming the action with a toothpaste tube.

Now inertia rises and that inner groan
of *not again*. Run hot water,
apply the white cream mask,
begin obediently under the right ear.
I could do this blind
and I suppose there's almost pleasure
in pulling the razor down
making that clean stripe, knowing
as I work there's not a stroke wasted
the reverie punctuated by my tap-tap-tap
on the basin-edge.

Here's one thing at least that can't be rushed
or else there's blood.
You're nicked!
So take the chin-work slow
draw upwards from the lip under the nose
repeat until the rasping goes.

Done. I wash the mask off
and allow a little patting down.
For the ten thousandth time
I am a smooth new man.

Touch the silence

Witching hour Yulara 4pm,
campground entry jammed
every wagon every caravan in this country
coughing up kids people diesel…
haven't they read on the entry pillar
Ayers Rock resort, touch the silence

somewhere out there
the spinifex body of red-sand silence

but not here
as car doors slam
buses spew out schoolkids on tour
kids kick footies
barbies are fired up
the earlybirds are into the dishes
and Yulara's generator throbs on and on…
we are in the dune-burbs
not touching the silence

though it tries a little, the silence
as the cold settles and people bed down
but the woman laughing like a banshee
it's the funniest thing she's ever heard
this silence and she's trying to rip it apart

and when she's finished it's me
on the pee-run it might be 2am
unzipping the silence zzzzp zzzzp zzzzzp

padding to the showerblock
past the shadow wagons the tent shapes
and I feel under the night generator's thrum
the body of red sand silence

possibly it touched me.

Narcissus is us

A baby learns it in the womb
the ringtone of its mother's phone
the hum in her bones
as she speaks
a baby learns the pleasure
the tap tap texting tremor
bliss of connection gurgled with milk
and soon its eyes are fixed on the face
it will love all its life

the screen
the screen
once hooked it'll never be weaned

the infant learns to finger-flick
as soon as suck its thumb
the toddler loves a toy that squawks
a thousand ways at its command
and soon they'll have a tablet all their own
and every kid must have a phone
their illuminated hand-held home

Narcissus is us
look into the pool
the surface bewitches
the shallows rule

admit it
you can feel the pull
the tentacles of Google
and you are gripped
by the need to know
the need to show
to share to blare to blow to be
connected

why bother waiting
check the lyrics
to the soundtrack of your life
right now
and get your breakfast pics on Instagram
slice by sourdough slice
so we can watch you eat

and follow you throughout the day
and follow you throughout the day
first in this place then in that
doing something with your cat
wearing clothes and having hair

and here's me with my special friend
here's my favourite coffee blend
here's me sleeping
here's me drunk
here's me wiping up some gunk

selfie-heaven here we are
a hundred thousand pics of me
and where I've been
and what I've seen
just check your screen while

firing tweets off everywhere
your endless riveting commentary
feeds and trends and bends and billows
the whole world is awash with blah
however near or far

and still I haven't mentioned blogs
I'd rather study moss on logs
not even dogs read blogs
the truth is you're a tiny cog
one facebook face among six billion

but so linked-in
to every humming thing
your camera talks to your phone
and the phone talks to the fridge
and your eyebrows switch on the lights
you're wireless, tireless

Narcissus is us
look into the pool
the surface bewitches
the shallows rule.

What's cooking?

we're going up

atmosphere skin-taut
with our endless exhalations
cars chimneys cows tundra
the balloon expands and expands
no adult hands in charge
no-one to put a knot in it

the sheerer the tighter the skin
the sharper the frisson
and the more gets pumped in
fires vapour breath hyperbole

as the planet-balloon approaches the pin
the childlike urge
is to see what happens

the overthinking and the heated minds

of humans since we busied ourselves
harnessing fire and burning and powering
whatever was hot at the time
and now the planet's caught our virus our inflammation
thrashing around with puffed cheeks and hills
and can't throw us off quickly enough
the drunken forests the weeping glaciers it was always
coming the fever the heat the feverishness
and where are the planet-doctors are they hiding
or have they given up seeing the condition is global
and can't be shaken off not this time the Anthropocene
and we strut the warm air and soak the heat up
avoiding surfaces that holler *hot* and keep talking
and thinking and overthinking and overtalking and
overheating and maybe sometime soon we'll see this
planet as the furnace the crucible the oven
so what are we cooking?

unmoored untethered glare

sun out to shock
                light in shards

even if the moon grows hot
                I will not lose my cool

trying out this new language
                jittery unpinned words

                          squinting into them

anxiety floodlit

brilliantly unseasonal

tipping point talk

we're tipping
          at talk point
talk as we tip
          at the point
we're about to tip
          we're sliding
we've slid
          we're falling
or boiling
          frogs in the pot
                    or what
is this the point
          is it tipping right now
will something come down
                    like a lid
and the flame
          will we feel it
or is that next year
          is that a crack
                    in the sky
looks that way

carbon copies

trailing petrol-breath
carbon residue on the tongue
eyes' rainbow sheen

feet wheels bodies engines
half petro half chemical
we burn fluently

worship the old carbon ancestor daily
having plundered his black bones from open-cut graves

we need him burnt
to glide about our lives
engines heads brains
always humming
            always running

        trailing petrol-breath
        carbon residue on the tongue
        our eyes' rainbow sheen

and tonight…

what's cooking?

whole embankments of wood-roasted cauliflower
heads rolled in ash California-style

injections of microbead foam
                              in acidic sea-broth

exquisitely foraged arctic leaves
snatched from the Caribou's mouth

the oily taste of petrochemical plants

diners stampeding
                         through sourdough streets

grease the buffers
                       as we run off the kitchen rails
fire the woks
        do phở
             swim against the rising tide of turmeric latte

the planet is cooking for you

the entire country inflamed

purple welt on the temperature chart
the beast from the Pilbara
has lumbered down for a look
seems he wants to fry your particular spot
the place you thought was temperate
no it's never happened before
this is off the chart get used to it
and don't get stirred up it creates heat
inertia is best: wrestle the beast
you'll end up floored his face cooking yours

*

days later when the creature finally slopes off
you realise the fridge has been left open
and your beer is warm and you've been imagining
all that time how cold the bottle would feel in your hand
the beast has stolen your notion of cold
go on say it *cold cold cold*
see it's just a word
was it ever a thing?

headlong (with Icarus)

in the rush in the rush in the rush towards
the freedom and fetch of the rush towards

like Icarus soars in the rush towards
we're all given wings in the rush towards

burnt by the sun in the rush towards
what use are our wings in the rush towards

down like a stone in the rush towards
warnings unheard in the rush towards

who watches over us in the rush towards
as everything melts in the rush towards

when the sea swoops up in the rush towards
wings meet water in the rush towards

in the rush in the rush in the rush towards
who watches over us in the rush towards

more more

eggs baked rolled truffled
smashed eggs with kale and avo
paleo-poached eggs from zen chooks
and all being eaten under the sun
like breakfast was the only season
and yellow on everyone's lips...
eat everything you can while you can
dab the yolk as it pools on your plate
go on break the membrane of the other one
the heat on your face is only the sun
poaching your skin at 11am
traffic and sourdough and butter oozing
go on eat for the city for the country
so long as the platefuls come
and the eggs are perfected
and the cool kids are serving
tomorrow there'll be more
that's where everyone's heading
that's what you're hearing
the sound of *more more*
and the sun dripping scorn
and the heat in people's cheeks
and all the eating the eating

flare

imagine this planet sporting a red halo
                               a spiky corona

you'll say the sun...

I say the earth this one
say it with the same queasy feeling I get
watching gas flared off

the carelessness of the flame

argue with me
say the planet's cloud-wrapped green
                              and from space it's living blue
an eye open in the blackness

I can't help this feeling
this mental trace of something inflamed
the planet's new outline

but where are the snows of yesteryear?

winter scene
some print from the seventies
a high country sweep of snow
granite ribs the buried memory
of Villon's words
his fingers on the spine

but where are the snows of yesteryear?

when snow had a grip

spooked

wouldn't you be spooked too?
you know like a horse pig-rooting its way
over the paddock white-eye-rolling

we're both spooked
by the writing in the sky
everything is over

horse looks one way I the other
panting eyes wild inconsolable
until we realise perhaps we got it wrong
the sky might read not *over*
but *clover* or even *lover*

febrile times this new era
signs piling up portents everywhere
and you who are not spooked
at the checkout in Bunnings
who are doing fine thanks very much

horse and I are astonished
at you carrying on
like nothing has happened
can't you see
it's done it really is over

look out to sea

remember innocence?
now more than a blue horizon line
it's an ocean restless and warm
with new power in its hands
a need to explore fresh territory
eyeing off your beach house
and New York Sydney Shanghai

if this doesn't cool your thinking
move to the hills and build up high
wave your millenarian banner
look down on all that roving surge
that watery expansion

history happens faster now

everyone racing all over the planet
                like their touchpaper's been lit
stand still they'll turn to stone
                trees have never looked so taciturn
limbs stripped off by the last cyclone/ hurricane
                another baleful eye on the weather map
so much energy to burn
                world chucking its clothes off
the haze we're making
                with our hot columns of molecules
torrents of data
                everything permeable
as we hurtle in carbon-fibre skins
                over the planet's curve
streaming downloading generating

heat: the new human phosphorescence

crowing

hard to ignore the conspiracy
                the black spots in my vision
corner of the eye where crows happen
                crow-shapes punched from sheet metal
arrayed on the fence
                or should that be arraigned
it's the template disturbs
                the black lacquered arrogance
like they know something
                the way they thrive
in a dirt paddock
                on the sniff of an old fence
on the lumped dead creatures
                we provide
with such crow-confidence in the future
                (the thing that frays in me
that unpicks my seams)
                they'll pick its brains
they already have
                the way they luxuriate in the heat
like they've dialled it up a notch
                for the shimmer off the road
as the records topple
                they lord it
I don't want to catch the crow eye
                it burns too brightly
a match to my paranoia
                the hopped-up confidence
staking out country
                the ubiquity of crow

so prove me wrong
                rewrite what I'm seeing
(at the corner of my eye
                under the radar)
tell me I'm imagining dark things
                that I've become crow-centric
have you seen any dead crows lately?
                I know what you'll tell me
they're Ravens
                Little Ravens
I won't be listening
                crow is what they are
stropping their beaks
                on sandpaper country
it's Eden we're creating for them
                and the emptier this world-box
rattling round with drought and fire and wind
                the better for crows
look at them glossed up
                the full pose
shaking a beard shuffling trousers
                several steps ahead of us
triumphalist
                pretending to be raptor
until the blunt head
                the fascist outline shows

crow
>	I don't exaggerate
though I should admire their gift
>	for increasing in spite of us
I've even seen the light
>	on a crow's overwing
now that's something shows mettle
>	until you hear what they're saying

it's not pretty

I'm not granite

I get drunk late one afternoon and feel more hopeful
when the ridges step off with some authority
and again this morning in the forest
fallen bark the colour of cinnamon
hyacinth orchids a waxy stippled pink

even if they build a perspex dome over everything
the trees will stay in cahoots
and keep talking

yes but for how much longer

it's not the question you should ask
Frank's cattle are behaving on the road
the bridge is doing its job
fences haven't failed overnight
houses are still standing
and the school bus is smack on time

the mountains have a certain look

                sitting further off and milkier
                as if prepared

Mt Palerang's granite eye open
I try holding it steady

and continue my day-mountain-sitting
under the enamel sky

night-mountain-sitting
day-mountain-sitting

held

    let go

held

In addition to being a poet Harry Laing is a comic performer and children's author. For many years, together with his partner, poet Nicola Bowery, he has co-led the popular PoetryAlive weekend workshops. He also runs writing workshops in schools and regularly performs for hundreds of schoolchildren. Harry lives beside Monga National Park near Braidwood on the Southern Tablelands of NSW.

Acknowledgements:

A number of these poems were published in *The Canberra Times, Cordite* and the anthology *The House is Not Quiet* and *The World is Not Calm, poetry from Canberra.*

*

My thanks to Ralph Wessman at Walleah Press for taking this book on.

And a very special mention to my partner and editor, Nicola Bowery.

www.ingramcontent.com/pod-product-compliance
Lightning Source LLC
Chambersburg PA
CBHW021156080526
44588CB00008B/359